DIMENSIONS

THE WORLD IN A 12-YEAR-OLD BOY'S EYES

YUHAN WANG

COPYRIGHT

CONTENTS

Dedication

This book is dedicated to my mom, for she accompanies me all the way along, and she is always with me when I am facing difficulties.

Acknowledgment

First, I'd like to thank my teacher Howard. He guides me into the door of writing, and I will never be able to publish my book without his help.

Second, I'd like to thank my family members. During writing these essays, I have had hard times, but all of them offer their help for me. Especially my brother, who gives my book a good name.

Third, thank you, my readers.

Prologue

Self-presentation

I am a twelve-year-old boy from China, and I am always optimistic, humorous, and hard-working.

English is one of my favorite subjects. Being bilingual is my goal. I read a lot, from novels such as Harry Potter, Lord of Rings, Kite Runner to historical books. After reading hundreds of books, I had the impulse of writing. Since I like logical things, I started to write persuasive essays. The topics are typically what I am curious about or the current affairs. How to look at the world from a teenager's point of view? I gave my opinions. I have kept on writing for two years, and I'm so proud and excited that my first book, which contains dozens of persuasive essays, will be published! Also, there are some novels by myself, and I hope you like them.

In school with the character of easy going and humor, I enjoy good relationship with my classmates. Since my academic scores are often the best in school, I have time to further develop my interest in Math. I participated in many math competitions both home and abroad. For me, Match is a kind of brain gymnastics that I enjoy very much.

Don't label me as a nerd. Actually, I'm quite good at sports as my classmates call me strong but nimble. I've been the class commissary in charge of sports for 6 years, and my passion lies in baseball and tennis. Speaking of baseball, I'm the team captain and the starting pitcher of the school baseball team. In the past four years, game after game. For me, baseball is not only a sport but also a tool to make friends and gain more scopes toward the world. Shenzhen, Qingdao, Hong Kong and New York, North and South Carolina witnessed me and my team's victories and failures. I enjoyed communicating with kids from other parts of China and the world through baseball.

I started to play tennis when I entered the primary school. Every week, I play twice or three times a week and this has lasted for six years. Tennis is fun but also tiring. My legs are always filled with iron after playing. However, I never give up. Sports not only make me healthy but also a way to build the character, and both baseball and tennis have already become part of my life.

Other than academic subjects and sports, I am a fan of wild animals and like to take photographs of them.

Finding leopards in Sri Lanka; birds and animal watching in Hong Kong, Shenzhen and other places in China…..they were fun times for me during the vacations. Beautiful animal pictures always give me great pleasure.

Here it is: this is me, a boy with great curiosity and passion for being a better self. Here, I sincerely hope all of my readers, no matter young or old, enjoy reading both my novels and my persuasive essays and enjoy seeing the world from a teenager's angle.

CHAPTER 1

The Discussion of Events & The Books I Like

All good things must come to an end

Everybody will be lucky sometimes, but will good things last forever? In my point of view, it won't.

Good things will be there sometimes, for example you win lottery. After you win, you will be very happy which may cause a lot of problems. When human beings feel happy, they can easily becoming relax which may result in being cheated or some other tragedies. Of course somebody will say: "But if I can control myself and stay alert, I can't be cheated." Yes, some people can control themselves, but they are only a few among us. The rest of us don't have such self-control, so we can become relax easily. Base on this, I think good things can't last long.

Let me give you an example: In China's Song dynasty, our poems and cultures went to a very high level. Everyday people sang and danced, they were very happy, but they forgot that the most important thing was defending their country. This caused the dynasty's end. At first, the people from other nationality called Jing attacked them, Song lost. It gave a lot of places to Jing and went to South. In South, Song continued to sing and play. At last, Song was defeated by Jing because of their joyful life.

This story tells us that a joyful life can destroy you, and that's why Steve Jobs said: "We must stay hungry!" Therefore, I think good things may happen, but it can't last long.

How Italy and China handle the outbreak of Coronavirus

The coronavirus is a worldwide pandemic and each country is fighting against it; however, each has its own way. Today, I will discuss Italy and China's plans for controlling the virus and compare them.

In early December, the coronavirus appeared in Wuhan. In these days, lots of people argued about whether the virus would spread quickly, but the local government ignored the virus. When Chinese New Year began, the virus grew worse. China locked down Wuhan completely, which meant nobody could leave his home. At the same time, Italy began to have some reaction by controlling Chinese entering Italy. From Chinese New Year to the beginning of March, life in China was in pause. No school, no work, everything was frozen. Almost nobody could leave his home. Due to this severe measure of lock down, in early March, coronavirus was under control. In the meantime, the situation in Italy was getting worse and the lock-down policy was also implemented there. However, it didn't help much. The infected amount and the death rate keep on climbing, even on present days.

In this peculiar time, the lockdown is proven to be a good choice. Why did China succeed but Italy failed? Actually, it was due to different types of government and different life habit. China has a very strong central government. One voice, others just listen and obey, this model means efficiency. Italy's government is more democratic. Arguing and debating are very common. However, the virus doesn't wait. Slower action cost Italy heavily. Moreover, Chinese are more reserved. We often shake hands on social occasions. Italians are warmer, and they hug and kiss much more than us. Unfortunately, these help the virus' spreading.

From the above we can say the same policy in different country leads to different result. Coronavirus is the common enemy of human beings. I sincerely hope Italy can win the battle as early as possible.

The cultural difference between east and west

We're facing a worldwide pandemic. Our lives have changed dramatically. However, when facing lockdown, one of the commands of the governments, people in different countries response in their own ways. The different reaction is caused by different culture, and I will discuss the cultural difference between east and west.

In eastern countries, when the government said lockdown, people obeyed and stayed at home as long as being told, but it's a different story in western countries. In my opinion, there are two main reasons: the saving habit and the characters.

Many people in west don't save money. This habit is formed during ancient times. The fathers of the western countries were hunters; they ate what they got that day and didn't save food. Back to these days, since they don't save money, they have to continue to work in order to live.   However, eastern countries are different. The majority of the easterners can be traced back to farmers in ancient times. They planted seeds in spring, worked in summer, harvest in autumn. The food they got had to support their whole year, so they knew how to save food. This habit affects the people these days, which can be reflected on our habit of saving money. With money in pocket, the easterners can stay at home longer than the westerners.

The second difference lies in characters. The westerners are more open, unrestrained while the easterners are more disciplined and reserved. This can also be explained by the difference between hunters and farmers. Hunting is more dangerous and unpredictable, while farming is more tranquil and consistent. Hunters may value happiness more than life. Lockdown means boring life, and they can't bear it.

This is the culture difference between east and west, so when others do something that we can't understand, don't jump to criticize; instead, try to figure out the reasons and accept them.

Positive & Negative Impacts of New Technologies

New technologies are double bladed swords. Each one has positive impacts and negative impacts. This can be discussed in three ways: telecommunication, advanced weapons and robots.

New technology helps us to communicate faster. If I have a friend in Amcrica, and I want to talk with him, I only need to call him on the telephone or internet; but if I want to talk with him a thousand years ago, maybe it will take a month to send a message to him. This is the convenience telecommunication gives us, it's a lot easier to communicate when we are far away, but it also has negative impacts, when we received a message a thousand years ago, we would be really happy because this was rare, but today, we may receive hundreds of messages in one day. When we greeted an old friend a long time ago, we would be excited, but now, you can communicate with him easily by we-chat, so we do not treasure it very much.

Usually, people think new technology make the war more terrible, but it may stop the war when the war is going to happen. Let me give you an example. If two countries had a quarrel in the past, they might have a war; but now, since both countries have new weapon such as nuke, that may avoids the war. Each country uses it to threaten the other, and both countries will be more cautious to start the war. However, sometimes it can be fatal too. If a country is autocratic, the leader is crazy, and they have nuke, nobody can sleep well at night. A city may be wiped out of the map after he fires the nuke only for fun. That is the negative impact.

Everybody should be familiar to the third one; it is robot. Robot can help human doing the job, which is tiring, boring and repeated. That can save lots and lots of labor; but it has disadvantage, Since the human may be replaced by the robots who have some things that human can never match, such as never tired, inefficient, non-mistakes, this may cause social problems.

A coin has two sides, and so is technology.

Three things that Money cannot buy

Money is the key to all doors, but it's not everything. There are three things that you can't get by money: they are time, wisdom and love.

Everybody says time is the most valuable thing in the world, and it cannot be bought. Time is fair to everybody, everything. It is a natural thing, and people cannot control it, so it does not have a price. You can save money, but you cannot save time. You can have lots of money by do not use them, but if you do not use time, it will never come back. You can get money from the others, but not time, and you can never know how many time have left in your life. Based on these facts, time is more valuable than money.

Many people know a story from Bible. One day, when King Solomon was asleep, God came in to his dream and asked him, "What gift do you want the most?" Solomon answered, "I want wisdom". You can see how important wisdom is. Wisdom is a kind of gift that life gives to you, and it is part of you. Nobody can rob it from you. It comes from knowledge and life experience. A war or a disaster may make you lose all your money, but they can't take your wisdom away. With the wisdom, you can create a miracle.

If we were robots, then everything we made have a price. But there is a difference between human and robot, it is love. If you are in the robotic world, your mum may sell you without hesitation if the buyer gives her a lot of money, but in the human world, your mum will never do this because of love. Love is precious, priceless so it can't be measured by money.

As you can see, money isn't everything.

What are some qualities that all great leaders possess?

In history, there are many great leaders. However, what are the qualities that all great leaders process? In my opinion, they are overcoming fear, taking risk, and taking care of talents all the time.

It is impossible to be a great leader without fear and risk. If it were possible, then anyone could have done it. However, it's not fear that makes a leader great; it's acting in fear that makes them great. When you are becoming more and more powerful, you will face more powerful opponents. Until one day, you and your biggest opponent are both standing on the highest peak and both of you are the mightiest. At that time, your fear will reach the highest point. However, only those who noticed the fear and still choose to risk everything can be the greatest. Winston Churchill serves as a good example. In WWII, when facing Germany that is far stronger than England, he overcame the fear and chose to fight.

A great leader always has the wisdom and talent of finding and digging out a genius. Great leaders care the ones who are employed, but they are more concentrated on the ones who really have dreams and goals because only the ones who have goals can help the leaders success. They can see the people who actually want to make the world better, but not the ones who just want money and high position. Great leaders can foresee what a man will become based on his qualities, but they do not care what the man is now. Nimitz, a five-star marshal in WWII, was found after the defeat of the Pearl Harbor by President Roosevelt, and at that time, Nimitz was only a HR manager. From this example, we can see Roosevelt was a great leader since he can find a genius, who can later become a great general, in the crowd.

In conclusion, the qualities that all great leaders have are being able to overcome fear and recognize talents. By doing these two things, they are able to success.

Is chess a sport or a game?

Chess is very famous around the world. Some people think it is a game, but some people think it is a sport. However, in my opinion, it is a sport, because chess has everything that other sports have.

A sport is which athletes train and compete with defined set of rules in exact fairness, while game is a competition with well-defined set of rules that tries to reach impartial.

Chess has well defined rules and the players need athletically training, so I think it is a sport.

If you want to play sports, you have to be well trained. You must spend lots of time practicing your skills for the sport. However, if you just play a game, you only need to obey certain rules. Soccer, for instance, is a sport. Players train for it and compete in a match. However, Poker, which is a game, you only need to learn the rules and then you can play, you don't need to train for it. For this reason, Poker isn't defined as a sport.

Chess is a sport because you have to train hard for it. Without being trained, you will lose definitely even if you know the rules. A chess game is both a competition of brain and mental, not just playing.

I'm a chess player and have played many chess games. When playing, I have to predict the next move of my opponent and try to figure out my best move; It involves logical thinking. While in a poker game, the winning depends heavily on the cards that you draw. As you can see, one of them is an exact fair game, but the other is by random.

If chess is defined as a game, then it means that an amateur may beat an old hand, this is impossible in reality. In poker, an amateur can be a winner if he draws good cards.

From this, we can conclude that chess is a sport.

The call of the wild

Today, I will tell you a book about animal, its name is "The call of the wild". The story is about a dog named White Fang. He has an amazing life, and I will tell you his story.

White Fang was a wild wolf. When he was young, he lived with his mother which was a dog. They lived with people and White Fang learned how to serve them. When he grew up, a man bought him and let him carry the sledge. At that time, everybody went to north for gold washing. Later, people sold their dogs to others. White Fang became a very good sledge dog during that period of time. At last, he was bought by a good man named Scott who trained White Fang from a wild creature to a home creature and from right to wrong, and the most important thing was he gave White Fang love.

After reading this book, I think love is the most powerful thing on earth. If you use power such as hitting or threatening to conquer a man, he will not obey you by heart. If you want to conquer a man in heart, you need to reform him, like what Scott did to White Fang, and the only to reform is love. A man giving love to others will be extremely happy because he gives happiness to others. He will be loved by people. There is a saying in China, which is giving others roses leaves fragrance in hands. Love is priceless, so giving love to others is an action full of nobility.

In the story, the author wanted to say that love was the most important thing in the world. I felt that in the story and agreed with the author.

Where the Red Fern Grows

"Miracles are created by you, not by anyone else." The book "Where the red fern grows" is about the adventures of a boy and his two dogs. It tells me the truth that love and real feelings can make miracles. Why do I say that? I will show you two pieces that support my opinion.

The first piece was about how they fought the mountain lion in a cave which was in the hills. "I never saw my dogs when they got between the lion and me, but they were there, side by side, they rose up like one." "There in the flinty hills of the Ozarks, I fought for the lives of my dogs." From these sentences, a picture appeared to me vividly, the boy swinging his axe, screaming crazily, tears running down his cheek, chopping the fatal, devil cat, the dogs rising like one, forgot about live and death.

Later on, one of the dogs died, what happened later on was very touching. The two dogs lived together since they were born, and the relationship between them was so strong that even they were in very different world, they cannot be separated. "I noticed how lifeless she was, I offered her food and drink, but she wouldn't even touch it." "I found her lying on her stomach, legs stretch out straight, front feed folded back." The dogs could not be separated, even by death. The dog was nearly dead, but with the last effort remaining in her body, she dragged herself to his grave. The two dogs finally stayed together forever.

In this book, two miracles happened. With a heart filled with anger, the boy fought the lion; with hearts that contained the loyalty to their master, the dogs fought the lion too. A little boy and two dogs killed a mountain lion, wasn't that a miracle? The ground under the big tree's leaves was not any special, but when the boy buried his dogs there, there grew up a sacred red fern. Why? Part of his spirit was buried there including the most excited part in the forest, the most memorable part in the Ozarks, and the most joyful part in his childhood. He loved his dogs so much, and for that, the sacred red fern grew.

The red fern existed not only on the mountain top, but also in the author's heart. It will always be there.

The Kite Runner

The door opened with a slow creak and I went in my room. I looked around and grabbed the book which I liked most. Its name was "The Kite Runner".

This book was mainly about Amir and his servant Hassan. They lived in Afghanistan which had the tradition of kite chasing. The two boys liked to read together. They had a great family and lived happily. One day, there was a fight between Hassan and another guy. Amir had two choices – help his friend or run away. He chose the latter because of fear.

From that time, a gap appeared in their friendship. At last, Hassan left Amir. After that, Amir's whole family went to America. Later Hassan died. He left his son, Sohrab, an orphan. Amir went back to Afghanistan to rescue Sohrab because of the deep guilt in his heart after that fight. At last, Sohrab began to adapt the new life because of the kite competition.

I think this book's best part is how Amir rescued Sohrab from the hopeless life. He fought bravely with the bad guy in order to bring Sohrab out of Afghanistan. He saved him physically. Later, he took him to the kite competition. He gave him the hope of life by the kite chasing and the sentence – For you, thousands of times, which Hassan had told him before.

From this book I think a real friendship can't be truly broken, although it suffers difficulty sometimes. The friendship will not only continue but also pass to the person who is connected with the friend. It's the connection between the two families. If we describe the events in this book as marbles, friendship is the string to connect them.

CHAPTER 2

Compare & Contrast

Relative fairness and absolute fairness

Should we take entrance exams to middle schools?

Being a 6th grader, I now face the crucial time of entering middle school. In China, students will be allocated to middle schools near home but students who are academically good seek for better schools and vice versa. However, should we have a test when we enter the middle school or should we just be distributed to the nearest school? In my opinion, we should have a test.

In my opinion, one of the important criteria of education is to provide student with suitable courses. By being tested, the students can be divided into several levels. In this way, the teachers can prepare the class more easily; they don't have to be puzzled with how hard the class should be. Similarly, the students don't have to worry about the quality of the class.

Having a test has many benefits as above, why does the government forbid it? It involves China's 9 years compulsory education, which emphasizes on fairness.

Actually, the facts above are connected to relative fairness and absolute fairness. Relative fairness is that the thing you get is based on how much you pay, but absolute fairness is that everyone is the same.

Relative fairness is like climbing a hill, if you are capable and willing to make effort, you can keep on climbing and get better view; if you are tired and unable to climb, you may stay or go down until the level is suitable for you.

Absolute fairness is like a lake with everyone being a drop of water. No matter how hard you jump, you will never be able to leave the lake, and the spray you make will help the others to live.

Absolute fairness and relative fairness have to be combined to use. If there is only absolute fairness, than no one will work hard since it is useless; if there is only relative fairness, than some people that are not smart will be abandoned.

In conclusion, we should allocate students to their nearest school in order to ensure fairness, and at the same time, give the geniuses a chance to have a test. By doing this, they can go to higher levels and not to be erased.

The differences and similarities between Burger King and Shake Shack

Shake Shack, the world's hottest burger maker; Burger King, one of the old guard and one of the uninspiring fast-food behemoths that is being disrupted. What is the differences and similarities between them?

The difference is Shake Shack looks modern, clean and inviting, but Burger King is dirtier and with windows covered with signs. Both restaurants are always busy with customers, but Shake Shack has a short and neat line; Burger King has a confusing and messy line. When you sit down in Shake Shack, you will notice that the seating area is full of light, and it looks clean and tidy; Burger King was not so well, swiveling chair and filed floor makes us feel bad.

But what truly matters is the burger. Actually, I haven't eat burgers in America's Burger King before, but only in China's. The burger there is really good. It is cheaper than Shake Shack's but bigger. Meat is very good; cheese is completely melted, and vegetables are fresh, but the calorie is higher too.

Based on the things I said, Shake Shack will cost more than Burger King, but that doesn't make any difference, everybody will pay 1 dollar more to have better environment and better service.

There are so many differences, but what about similarities? To tell the truth, I don't find any similarities. I think it's mainly because they are in different times. When Burger King is hot, Shake Shack doesn't even exist. The old store is getting worse, and the new store is getting better, that's how everything works.

These are the differences and the similarities between Burger King and Shake Shack.

The similarities and differences between black hole and white dwarf

Black hole is a super-giant monster searching food in the universe, while white dwarf is a useless rock floating in the universe lonely, what is the difference and similarities between them?

There are three main differences between them: the way they are born, the way they live, and how they die. When a star is dead, if its mass isn't big enough, it will turn into a white dwarf; however, if a star's mass is big enough, it will have a huge explosion and turn into a new form which is a neutron star or a black hole. For example, when our sun is dead, it will only become a white dwarf since its mass is too small compared to the star becoming a black hole, which has to be one hundred times heavier than the sun. In the life of black hole, it inhales everything that comes near it, and makes itself larger and more powerful. However, the white dwarf exists more like a meaningless rock floating in the universe. The last difference is how they die. After a google years swallowing, a black hole will explode; however, the white dwarf will not die, it will cool off and become dark. Gradually, it will turn into a metal ball, waiting to be crashed or swallowed.

The only similarity I can find is they both have big mass. Black hole has big mass is proved by its huge gravity, and white dwarf also has big mass. Do you know that a white dwarf which is as big as a house has the same mass of earth?

That's the differences and similarities between black hole and white dwarf, a swallower and a free man.

What Are the Similarities and Differences Between Rocks and Minerals?

Minerals are beautiful and special, but rocks are just something usual on the ground. However, rocks and minerals are both solid, stable and being found in the earth. What are the similarities and differences between them? In my opinion, the similarities are they aren't manmade and alive; the differences are minerals are beautiful and valuable while rocks are the opposite.

Rocks and minerals are both natural-made. They are formed in the way of complex geological processes, and also, they are not living organisms, which means they are not reproducing on their own. Rocks and minerals are both underground things found throughout the world. They occur on every continent and exist on many natural Earth surfaces.

Compared to the similarities, the differences between minerals and rocks have a bigger amount. Minerals are generally lighter in weight and more colorful than rocks. They vary a lot in colors, from white, yellow, to black and even transparent. Minerals not only have high value for their beauties, but they are also used in different fields since minerals have defined chemical compositions and ordered atomic structures. For example, uranium is used in nuclear weapons, gold in decoration and copper in industries.

Rocks, unlike minerals, are darker, harder and can only be used in the industries. Being different from minerals, all the rocks can be divided into three basic forms, which are sedimentary rocks, extrusive rocks and metamorphic rocks. Rocks are not as useful as minerals, but their heavy weights, hard structures and their huge amounts make them perfectly suited for use in the industrial and construction. For thousands of years, rocks have been mined from beneath the Earth's surface and removed to make roads, build bridges and create structural foundations for homes, offices, libraries and other buildings.

In conclusion, the similarities between minerals and

rocks are they are both natural-made and not living, and the differences are minerals are more colorful and have higher value in many different fields, and rocks are not that pretty and have narrower uses.

The differences and similarities between coffee and tea

Nowadays, when we are tired and sleepy, we often think about tea and coffee. The confrontation between the west and the east often appears in our life. However, what are the differences and similarities between them?

There are three main differences, which are the place they originated, the way they are made, and their color. A long time ago, a herdsman in west found some odd fruits. He ate them and became high-spirited. He gathered lots of this fruit and put them into his cup when he drank water. That is the embryonic form of coffee. In the 11th century, the Arabs began to plant bean on purpose, and in the 16th century, the Arabs brought coffee to Europe through Venice and the coffee became popular later on. Chinese began to drink tea thousands of years ago, but they planted them in their own gardens. In Tang Dynasty, which was about the 7th century, people began to plant tea trees in certain public areas and equal the harvest. When we drink coffee, we crush the coffee beans into powder and pour in water. Tea is different. We just have to pour water and put some dry tea leaves in. Coffee is usually black if you don't pour anything in, but tea is transparent with a little color.

There are three similarities between them. The first similarity is they can both make you not sleepy since both of them have some special chemical ingredients inside them, caffeine and theine. Furthermore, they both have bitter taste. The second difference, to tell the truth, is they are both drinkable. The third difference is both of them have many flavors. These two drinks are so popular in the world, so both of them have many different types. For instance, tea is separated into red tea, green tea and else; coffee is separated into black coffee and coffee with milk such as mocha, cappuccino and else.

These are the differences and similarities between these two drinks, a fashion of west and a culture of east.

CHAPTER 3

Persuasive Writing

Animals shouldn't be used in circuses or zoos

Nowadays, when we watch a show in a circus or in a zoo, we see some animals appear in the play, and they do something very interesting and funny. However, should animals be used in a zoo's or circus' show? In my opinion, they should not since they should be protected, and they will be harmed in the zoo.

The reason of why we should protect the animals is the protection of animals means the protection of human beings. Actually, our lives depend on animals a lot. The great scientist Einstein made a prophecy, which humans could only live three years longer after the distinction of bees. That proves the importance of animals. Animals also connect with nature. If a bird is extinct, like Dodo, a kind of plants will be extinct with it. Furthermore, if an animal's amount decreases fast, the ecosystem will be broken. For instance, if lion disappear in Africa, lion's prey will become a big problem since no animal can hunt them. Based on all the facts above, each animal should be protected since they are all important in the nature's ecosystem.

However, animals can't get the treatment they are meant to have. The purpose of someone who opens a circus is earning money, and the rarer the animals are, the more money they can get from the audience. Therefore, the boss will do whatever he can in order to get some precious animals. Furthermore, for making more money, animals are to be over used. When animals can't afford any performance longer, the boss will throw these old animals into wild. However, the animals' hunting skills are lost during the time in the circus or zoos. Therefore, they are doom to die in the wild. Overall, animals are not treated well.

In conclusion, animals shouldn't be used in circuses' or zoos' shows since they are meaningful for us; also they, like we human beings, are the creatures in nature and shouldn't be used for our own purpose.

Climate change is not constant and natural

Climate change is a big problem these days, and scientists are trying to figure out how to solve it. However, is climate change constant and natural? In my opinion, it isn't because firstly some events can change the climate abruptly, and secondly, carbon dioxide makes the atmosphere's concentration change that cause the change of the climate, and most of the carbon dioxide is manmade.

Everyone knows dinosaurs and we wonder why they disappeared from the Earth. It's commonly believed that a small planet hit the earth and caused the extinction of dinosaurs. When the planet hit the earth, volcanoes erupted and earthquakes happened. More importantly, dust from the volcanoes stayed in the air and covered the sun for a long time. All plants that depended on sunlight for energy died. This made the grass-eating dinosaurs have no food, and the death of the grass-eating-dinosaurs made the meat-eating dinosaurs lack of food. Eventually, dinosaurs disappeared. From this, we can see how a sudden event changed the climate abruptly.

Climate changing can also happen because of the greenhouse effect. When sunlight reaches the earth, some light is reflected back into space, while some light is absorbed and turn into heat. The heat is later on reflected by greenhouse gases into any directions and warms the earth. However, on Earth, human activities are changing the natural greenhouse. When the fossil fuels, such as coal or oil, are burning, this process combines carbon with oxygen in the air to make carbon dioxide. Since the last century, the burning of coal and oil has increased the concentration of the carbon dioxide in the atmosphere and therefore the greenhouse effect is strengthened. As a result, more and more heat can't escape back into the space. Therefore, the earth gets warmer and warmer. Based on the facts, global warming isn't natural.

In conclusion, some events can seriously change the climate, and human activities also play important role. Therefore, climate change is not constant and natural.

Some people think that in order to produce a happy society, it is necessary to ensure that there is only a small difference between the earnings of the richest and poorest.Is this right or wrong?

Everyone hopes for a peaceful and happy society; therefore, some people say that in order to reach this goal, it is necessary and important to ensure that the difference between the rich and the poor is small. However, in my opinion, this is not proper since by doing this, people's passion for working will decrease and the society will be in stagnation.

Everyone is different, both physically and mentally. Therefore, some people are rich, some people are poor. If the government makes every people have similar earnings, then the people who have more talent and capacity on working will be discouraged. He will think since the earning is more or less the same, it's unnecessary to work hard. His passion of working will disappear. If more and more people think in this way, the society will be inevitably becalmed.

From 1960 to 1970, China advocated equalitarianism. At that time, the entire farm field in the countryside belonged to collective community. Everybody farmed and got almost the same amount of earning no matter doing how much work. Therefore, everyone became lazier and lazier. The community was on the edge of broke. Farmers could hardly stay away from hunger. Then, Deng Xiaoping, who was one of the most important men in new China's history, changed the condition. He gave lands to farmers themselves. The earnings of the farmers depended on how much effort they put in. In this case, everyone's potential was brought out in order to get harvest. China's countryside became more prosperous. From this example, we can draw the conclusion that working for individual is the best way to ignite one's potential. When everyone is working hard, the society will make rapid progress.

In conclusion, the government shouldn't make the richest and the poorest have nearly equal earnings because this policy will hinder the development of the society.

Is it ethical to breed animals to get combined hybrids?

Animals are friends of human beings, and in China's ancient times, animals are the most important thing for most of the people. For example, horses for riding, cows for farming. However, some people breed different kinds of animals to get combined hybrids. Is this ethical or not? In my opinion, it is not ethical because of two reasons, which are use and respect.

First, there is no use to get combined hybrids any longer. For the ancient people, be full and alive were the most important things to do, so ethical code was put into the second position. In China's history, the most important hybrid was the combination of horse and donkey, which was mule. The biggest use of it was carrying heavy stuffs. It gathered the gene of horse and donkey, so this specie could run faster than the donkey and carry heavier stuffs than the horse. However, mules are useless nowadays. One truck can substitute a dozen of donkeys easily, no matter in speed or in carrying stuffs. Human's technology is continued improving. Till today, there are lots of machines. They can do most of the tiring stuffs while combined hybrids are made for these works that human cannot or don't want to do. Therefore, the excuse of getting combined hybrid no longer exists.

Moreover, making an animal in A specie to marry an animal in B specie is a great disrespect. If someone tells you marrying a monkey, what will you do? Maybe hit him hard, and lead to a big fight. This is just something on mouth. If someone is really forcing you to marry a monkey, then what will happen? Other animals are also living creatures; they should be respected as human beings. Therefore, it is really disrespecting the animals when forcing them in order to get combined hybrids.

In conclusion, no matter from the angle of use or respect, it is always not ethical to get combined hybrids.

Listening to music makes doing homework faster

Students have lots of homework to do, so is there a way for us to do homework faster? In my opinion, listening to music is one of them; because it offers relax when we are exhausted in doing homework.

I, a sixth grader, always have lots of homework to do, and it takes a long time to finish. When I am tired, I prefer listening to soft music. When the music is on, it feels like breeze which blows away my fatigue. When I finish listening some songs, I'm recharged and can again focus on my works.

Somebody may think music is a distraction when we are concentrated on doing homework, because if we focus on two different activities at the same time, then none of them will be finely done. In my opinion, music isn't a distraction. Our brain is separated in two parts: left and right. Left part is the place for knowledge, and the right part is the place for art. When we are doing homework, it is our left brain working, but when we are listening to music, it's our right brain working. It isn't a distraction, but mutual promotion instead.

In my school, when we recite some classical poems, our teacher always provides background music. She says music is helpful for us to remember the poems. I agree with that because music is the activator for memory. The great Einstein did the same thing. When he was working on some tremendous equations, he listened to music or played violin.

In conclusion, listening to music when you are doing homework isn't a distraction but a helpful habit indeed. Therefore, I agree with the topic.

Many people argue that eating junk food has led to an unhealthy lifestyle. This problem has become more common among young people these days. Do you agree or disagree that junk food is the cause of the issue?

In modern days, the life pace of young people is increasing in a fast speed. The work gets tiring, so the time for eating is lessened. Therefore, fast-food restaurants, such as burger king and McDonald, become very popular. However, are these restaurants, which are defined "junk food restaurants" by many adults, lead people to an unhealthy lifestyle? In my opinion, it does since junk food is bad for our health and it might become a habit of people.

Eating junk food is definitely bad for health. Compared with steamed meal, junk food are more fried, baked and roasted, while healthier meal are more often boiled. However, based on the science facts, fried and baked foods contain more fat than the boiled food if using the same ingredients. For example, Burger King sells food such as burgers, fries, cola and ice creams. These are delicious in my eyes but unhealthy in my mom's eyes. The fact is if someone has these foods for dinner every day, he will become a fat person for sure, which will lead to many diseases.

Also, eating junk food might become a habit. When I face the choice of eating French fries, fried chicken wings and hamburgers or eating boiled vegetables and meat, I will surely choose to eat the former even if they are junk food, and I think most of the people may have the same choice. The reason is simple, because they are more flavored. Gradually, you may be seduced to junk food.

In conclusion, junk food will lead to an unhealthy life style since it is not healthy and most of the people will be addicted to the junk food if getting used to it.

Technology has advanced tremendously over the past decade, so one can do so much with a mobile phone nowadays. Some people deem that children should not be allowed to own a personal mobile phone until they reach a certain age. Do you agree or disagree? If you do, what is the appropriate age for someone to begin owning a mobile phone?

Now, mobile phone is a part of our lives, because there is lots of our personal information and apps on the phone. However, phones are used not only for keeping information and contacting others, but also a chance for young people to play video games. So a question appears, can the children own a mobile phone by themselves? My opinion is no.

When a child opens a mobile phone without the guidance of his parents, he is possibly be tempted by the games which are finely made by psychologists and experts. He will think, "I will play only once and only a few minutes." After he starts, time just flies. Being a child with limited ability of self-control, how can he gain the upper hand with a bunch of smart game inventors who try their best to grasp the attention of players? Like smoking, playing video games will become a habit of yours. You will play more and more as if been bogged down in mud and cannot help yourself. This is a dangerous signal, which means you are immersed by games.

When you reach the above stage and still don't pay attention to it, you will do something weird with the force of your habit of playing video games. I know it sounds crazy. How can a habit make you to do something? Actually, it can. Don't underestimate the power of habit, because I was once a victim. For nearly a year, I couldn't resist the temptation by playing games every night. Every time when I touched my phone, I had a great amount of happiness although I knew it was a waste of time. Later on, with the help of my parents, I gave it up.

Base on the above, I think it's improper for children to own phones. However, when they are over 15 years old, they should be allowed to have phones. At that age, they've already in the high schools which are usually boarding ones. They need to contact their parents from time to time, and more important, they are more self-controlled.

In conclusion, a child shall not have his own phone, and he can have it when he reaches the age of 15.

Obesity is a serious problem and how to solve it

In modern days, due to the affluence of the society, the percentage of obesity is increasing, especially in rich countries. However, what are the things that will happen if the society is fulfilled with fat people and how can we solve these problems? In my opinion, there may result in two social problems which are low efficiency of productivity and high medical spending. The ways to solve it are to educate people eat less and exercise more.

First, having many fat people will cause the decrease of productivity. When obesity is severe, the society is filled with fat people. In most of the cases, fat will result in slowness in action, easiness for fatigue. Let's imagine, if a fat man and an ordinary man apply for a job in a factory, the second one will have more possibility to be hired since the boss may worry that the fat man isn't agile enough. From this example, we can see that if the society has many fat people, then many places, such as factories, will be less productive. Thus, the advance of the society will be slower.

The second problem is medical services. According to the data released in the media, in China in 2003, among serious diseases such as tumor, cancer, diabetes, Angio-cardiopathy, nearly 73% were caused by fatness. Some diseases, like high blood pressure, are unhealed, but the patient's losing weight is helpful. We can draw conclusion from the above that obesity is harmful to our health. Furthermore, it will increase burden to the patient's family due to high medical bill and care for the patient. Obesity will affect not only a single person, but also the family behind, and even more, the whole society.

If obesity is a serious problem, what is the way preventing it? In my opinion, the government should tell the citizens the serious consequences   of being fat, and advocate people to exercise more instead of lying on sofa and eat more healthy food instead of junk food. However, Rome is not built in one day and exercise has to be persistent. When a fat person keeps on exercising and controls his eating, he will definitely lose weight and become fitness.

In conclusion, obesity will cause productive and medical problems, and the ways to solve them are to exercise more and eat less junk food.

Poverty is a serious problem globally. Should governments be held responsible for this, or should this be seen as a result of people's own doing?

People worship money, because without it, life will stick. Everybody works to acquire it. However, poverty was still a big problem, because the amount of money that people earn is not equal. I think government shouldn't be held responsible for it, because people should create their own future.

In China, every kid has got nine-year compulsory education. The richest man in Asia Li Jiacheng and a beggar could both come from poor families and went to the same school. However, one of them wanted to change his situation so he was hard working, but the other thought he was already poor, so he didn't even try. The attitude and the effort of individual is the basic reason of the later on life. Being poor or not is based on yourself, not the government.

If the government over-subsidies the poor and makes them live as comfortably as hardworking people, when time passes, everyone will become lazy, because no matter how lazy you are, you will just have the same lives. Until one day, the government gives away all its money, the whole society will be in chaos. People will miss the lost easy-coming comfortable lives and unwilling to accept the hard-working style.

If the glory of the successful life comes more from individual than government, it will lead to different result. A kid with nothing left from his parents can become rich if he studies and works hard. Actually, everybody is nearly same smart, your achievement is mostly based on how hard you learn or work. None of the governments can help you with this.

In conclusion, the government should not hold responsible for the poor. There is a saying, "God helps those who help themselves." So, the way to reduce the poor is making everybody working hard.

Should horse racing be banned?

Horse racing is very popular; however, should horse racing be banned? In my opinion, it should since if a horse becomes a racing one, its whole life will be ruined.

Horses are meant to live in the wild. You can see them running around on boundless fields with large groups. However, racehorses often have to live alone in small rooms and can only get outside for training or races. This means they can never actually get to be free and will never know the feeling of no strings attached.

Horses are pushed to their limits in every race. They may even break a couple of bones during a race, due to high pressure, without noticing. Since the time between races isn't enough for them to fully heal, their body will become worse and worse. Until one day, they cannot afford racing anymore, and they will collapse. When the horse cannot race anymore, retiring can even be a mirage. Most horse owners will sell the horses to others.

Some of the solutions that are used when horses are injured badly are drugs, which can make the horses unable to feel great pain. These drugs allow horses to ignore their injuries for a little while and keep on running. However, this will make their injuries to be worse and finally to a point of no return that they eventually die. Furthermore, let a perfectly healthy horse eat drugs will also wear them down a lot faster and badly damage its body.

In conclusion, horse racing will make serious damage to the horse. Horse is a living creature like us, so their life should be respected like we respect human's life. Therefore, I think horse racing should be banned.

Should all students, from elementary school to high school, wear uniforms?

Every child has to go to school, and each school has its own uniform. Do students have to wear it? I agree with the statement.

School is a big family for students. If you see somebody wearing your school's uniform outside the school, you feel dear. If he doesn't wear it, maybe you can't recognize him, and he will be unfamiliar to you. Imagine this, you are in your school, and see lots of different colors and pictures surrounding you, you can't concentrate on learning, and you won't think this is a school. It seems like they are here because they want to have class but not because they are your classmates.

Let me give you an example. Once, my school gave us a chance of spring outing. All of us wore different clothes and used different backpacks. When we entered the park, we separated immediately. I found out a serious question, which was I couldn't find anybody. I searched for my classmates for a long time, and I found them at last. But the funny point was they were beside me for a long time. The second time it was better. All of us wore same clothes, and we were bright and shinning in the crowd. We could always find others because of our uniforms.

My school has done better than other public schools. Our uniforms are completely different with them. We have different colors such as yellow, red and green, and moreover they are comfortable and pretty. This allows us to be unified and diversified. We can choose our own colors. For me, when I am happy, I choose red; when sad, green. But pants are the same, this still makes us feel that we are in the big family of our school.

Based on the things I've said, I agree with the statement.

Should students go to school in summer?

Because of the pandemic, no one goes to school in these days. However, should students go to school in summer? In my opinion, we should since we have to finish the assignment of the year.

Why is finishing the assignment so important? The reason is that each school has already decided what to teach, so when some part is left behind, it will surely affect the later teaching. For example, if fraction is left behind these days, everything connected to fraction will be very hard to understand, or even can't be understand. If some important grammar details are missed, the test later will be a mess. Therefore, finish the assignment is rather important.

Although we are having online class, we will still have something left behind since having class face to face has more time and has more quality. For example, when I have class in school, each class has 40 minutes and there are 7 classes a day; however, when I have class online, each class has 30 minutes and there are only 4 classes a day. This shows the different amount of time. The quality is different too. First, when you have class in school, the teacher can know whether you are listening or not and can communicate with you, such as asking you questions or tells you to read, but neither of these two can be done. If you don't understand something, you can't ask your teacher, but think yourself. Above all, the effect of face-to-face is far better than having class online, so you have to spend more time on learning for getting the same result, which is learning in summer.

In conclusion, we should learn in summer, for we don't want to leave anything behind to make confusion in later learning.

What people do is the main but not the only cause of global warming

Nowadays, global warming has become a very serious problem, and everybody is trying to solve it. However, is global warming completely caused by man? In my opinion, people's doing is the main cause but not the only cause since there are natural causes.

Man-made causes do the most damage to the planet. For example, pollution is one of the biggest man-made problems. Pollution comes in many shapes and sizes, and burning fossil fuels is one thing that causes it. Fossil fuels are made of organic things such as oil. When fuels are burned they give off poisonous gas. Also, digging coal and oil allows methane, which is greenhouse gas that keeps heat in the earth's atmosphere, to escape. Methane is naturally formed in the ground, when oil is mined, a little bit mud has to be dug up. Along with it, methane is dug up too. Another major man-made cause of Global Warming is population. More people mean more food and more transportation. These bring more methane since there will be more burning of fuels.

However, natural causes also produce global warming. One is the release of methane from freezing land and wetlands. Another natural cause is that the earth goes through a cycle of climate change, which can usually last about 40,000 years. However, the speed that the natural causes affect the earth is far slower than the man-made causes.

In conclusion, both man and nature cause global warming, but man-made causes' damage is far bigger than natural's. Therefore, I agree that man-made causes is the main reason of global warming, but I don't think it is the only reason.

Should books portray the world as it is or as it should be?

We are very busy every day, going to school, doing our homework make us fully occupied. Books help us learn, but not hurt our feelings. Books shall portray the world as it shall be, and they need to show us the beautiful and the reasonable part of the world. I will use three types of men to explain my opinion.

First, if somebody is very sad, and he doesn't know what value he has. At that time, he reads a book which says, "there are too many useless men in the world!" what will he think? Maybe the book is true, but the reader can decide his own life and spend his life happily, these words in the book will make him feel worse, and the words may destroy his whole life. He is already very sad, so give him some positive energy.

Second, everybody has bad thoughts in his heart. When he reads a book which writes about the evil things, it may bring the potential terrible thought into reality. In this way, our world will become uglier.

Third, if somebody decides to chase the happiness in the world, when he reads the ugly things of the real world, he may be puzzled, and may think the thing he tries to seek is only a dream which is impossible to come true.

If the books only show the real society, many people will lose their ways, but what if the books show what a society should be? In Ming Dynasty, there was a famous philosopher called Wang Yangming. When he was young, he dreamed to be a wise man when he was young, but he couldn't find the right way to reach his goal. He tried several times and several ways such as finding the logics in the development of creatures, and he even locked himself in a stone coffin to think about philosophy. Once he was exhausted from tiredness and he grabbed a book to read. The book was about what a perfect world was like. Wang Yangming puzzled from a moment and suddenly knew how to become wise.

Our lives are fully occupied, so don't let the books cause

the suffering. Based on these, I think the books should portray the world as it should be.

The pros and cons of making school year-round

Vacations are the favorite times for the children since in that period of time children can play around, read whatever they like and travel around to explore the world. However, there are still voices that advocate the children to abandon the vacations and study year-round. What are the pros and cons of this arrangement? In my opinion, the advantage is the students can have more time to study; the disadvantage is it may cast shadow on childhood.

The obvious advantage of cancelling the vacations is the children have a bigger amount of time to study. As a child goes from elementary school to middle school and to high school, there are more and more subjects we need to study and the study go spirally more difficult. It requires us to spend more time. Cancelling vacations are definitely helpful with the study. Also, by keeping on doing exercises, you will have the feeling or instinct for the right answers. This is very similar to playing musical instruments. My brother used to play bassoon before, and his teacher told him to practice every day no matter it was holiday or not since if he doesn't, the sound he make would be different from the usual sound. In the track of study, each day we move forward and resting is the biggest enemy of study.

However, if the children study all year round, they may feel mentally and physically exhausted. This can lead to unhappy and unsatisfied childhood. In the case above, the children live in a single and unchanged model of studying hard every day. They lose the chance of going outside to feel and see the world. Finally they become study machines. The only thing they have and care for is high scores, but what they lose is a healthy body and happiness which is far more important in their lives. Furthermore, when they grow up, the childhood in the memories will be full of sorrow instead of happiness. In my eyes, this is definitely not worthy.

In conclusion, the pros and cons of study all year round are having more time for learning and having a tiring and tortured childhood, and in my opinion, I firmly disagree to cancel the vacations. Slow down and let us grow up in a natural way.

Some parents allow their teenage children to live independently, away from home. Other parents don't want their teenage children to live away from them. Which is better?

In modern days, many children think it is good to live on their own when they are just a teenager. They think they can have more freedom and can enjoy themselves while being alone. However, is living alone a good choice, or is it better to live with the parents? In my opinion, teenagers should still be on their parents' side because teenagers need guidance.

No matter in which period of time, having somebody on your side to point out your mistakes is always good, especially in transition periods. From elementary school to middle school is a big change. When going through it, having parents on the side is helpful. In middle school, there are more and more stuffs to learn, so some bad habits formed in elementary school have to be corrected. However, no one can help you to get rid of these bad habits when being along. Therefore, a student may get into the wrong way and no one is reminding him what should and shouldn't do. For example, my mom often helps me to get rid of bad habits and form the good ones. Before, I did different kinds of homework at the same time, which would decrease the efficiency. After the help of my mom, my speed of doing homework improves a lot.

Furthermore, most of the teenagers cannot control themselves from the temptation of playing video games or something like that. When your pals are studying, and you are playing video games, then how can you get along with him? Especially teenagers are in the time of not listening to anybody, so it is important to have somebody continuing to remind. Still, I will use myself as an example. When I was a fifth grader, I was satisfied with my score in my elementary school. Therefore, I was indulged in playing video games, and I even get up at midnight in order to play. However, I was captured by both of my parents and stopped doing these things. What if I don't have my parents on my side? Then I may play for the whole night, and finally, my score will decrease.

In conclusion, the teenagers should be on their parents' side since it is important to be on the right track and not doing some wrong things and parents can help doing these things.

CHAPTER 4

Fictional Writing

The Swallowers

The colonel, who was the highest officer in the spaceship, stood in the control cabin. His eyes stared at the mysterious universe. He looked solemn because he knew the task on his shoulder. His fleet, with the name of "The Defender" flew around the earth. They haven't met big challenges yet, only some meteorites floating in the universe. His fleet forced them to change direction when they were heading to earth. This wasn't hard for an advanced fleet, but today, he had uneasy feeling, just then, something came into his sight.

It was like a crystal ball of normal size, spinning fast, on the orbit to the earth. The colonel followed this strange ball, trying to figure out what it was. He ordered the metal arm of the spaceship to grab it and send it inside. As soon as the ball was in the cabin, it suddenly became foggy, and then a beautiful girl slowly appeared. She cried, "Warning! Warning! The swallowers are coming."

The colonel asked, "Who are you?"

"I am the only survivor of the planet the swallowers has just eaten."

"The what?"

"The swallowers."

"What are swallowers?"

"Swallowers are big, ugly creatures. Swallowers spaceship, or you can define it as their planet, looks like a big tire. Its width is almost 18,000 km wide. It can swallow a planet into the middle of it in order to get everything from it. The process usually lasts one century. When they finally let go of the planet, you can not recognize it anymore. The planet will go back to its baby form with no creature, no air or water, only hard rocks and lava."

"How horrible! It's like eating cherries, isn't it? Flesh is gone and only the nutlet left."

"Exactly! When our planet was swallowed, everybody felt as if he was floating, that was because of the gravity the tire made. All things began to move to that direction until they disappeared in their "mouth". I was the only one who escaped their gravity thanks to this crystal ball."

"Where are the swallowers?"

"They are just following me, heading for earth."

When the colonel was still thinking about whether the girl should be believed or not, suddenly, something came into his sight. The colonel used a few minutes to figure out that it wasn't a meteorite. It looked like a metal old pot, which was left in the dessert for a century, rusted and shaggy. It moved really fast!

However, the colonel felt uneasy, since there was a bad news, which was the swallowers technology was far better than the human being. The colonel decided to send a dozen of bombs to that " meteorite", but after a dazzling white light, all the bombs vanished. A voice was heard, "I'm the ambassador from the Swallowers. Send me to earth." The colonel had no choice but to obey.

When the pot-like spaceship landed on earth, important officials have been waiting there for long. A huge

dinosaur like creature came out. It was the ambassador，

who introduced his name as "Bunger", but based on the things he did afterwards, people later on called him "Butcher". Butcher walked toward the crowd. His every step made a huge noise.

"Hello little, cute bugs," Butcher smiled, "we have years to live together. I hope we will like each other." His sound was like a dozen of old train whistling.

One of the officials asked, "Dear ambassador, could you tell us the purpose of your planet heading to earth?" Although he spoke loudly, but it was still like flies squeezing compared with Butcher's voice. Butcher suddenly roared, "The great swallowers are going to eat earth, to continue its delightful journey."

"So what's human's fate?"

"That's what I'm going to decide today." When Butcher finished, he grabbed an official and threw him into his mouth from 5 meters away. It happened in a sudden; everyone was as dumb as a piece of wood. Only the bones' cracking sound was heard. A few seconds later, Butcher popped out that man's clothes, but nothing more. This made others remembering the scene when people were eating peanuts. Silence fell on the crowd.

The silence lasted for minutes, and suddenly, Butcher spoke, "Congratulation, bugs. I think you taste very delicious, but we are more interested in earth. I'll give you 48 hours to decide."

Every high official gathered. The discussion was heated. The colonel insisted to fight against the swallowers although the earth's technology was far less advanced than the swallowers. "Earth is our home. We have to try our best to protect it from the invaders. Be courageous, I have a plan." He described it and everyone agreed. However, somebody said, "Fighting means death. We should try once more to negotiate with Butcher."

Butcher's spaceship landed again on the earth at a ruins of an ancient city. He saw welcome flowers and food. A band was playing joyful melody. Two officers came and gave him a huge picture book, which was about human history. They said, "dear ambassador, there were so many creatures on this beautiful blue planet. After reading this book, we hope that you make a different decision of our fate. You see, this ancient city was newly discovered, and it was proved being the first city existed. Are you really planning to destroy a civilization which has being lasted for 6000 years?"

Butcher simply had a glimpse of the book and spoke, "Bugs, I'm fully not interested in this old ancient city, instead, I'm interested in the mud which was dug out."

Butcher put some extremely small things on his grant paw. It was ants, some were dead, and some were still crawling. A sympathetic expression appeared on his face. He said, "You showed me this ruins in order to gain my sympathy. However, your action actually harmed groups of other creatures."

The two officers looked puzzled.

The peaceful persuasion failed. Human decided to fight, using the colonel's plan.

Human decided to surrender. They told Butcher that

they wanted to leave the solar-system by using the moon as the spaceship and the nuclear as the energy. Butcher agreed.

However, the real plan was secretly making spaceships that could reach the light speed in order to escape the solar-system. The selected human beings with the important things of the civilizations on the earth will take the spaceships to try to find a new home for human beings in the universe. In the meantime, the colonel and his army were busy planting nuclear on the moon with the secret purpose of using it to destroy the "tyre", which was coming to the earth.

The day of leaving the moon has come. Butcher landed on the moon, because he wanted to say goodbye to human, not sincerely, but in a mocking way. The colonel and his army greeted him politely. Butcher noticed something unusual: a few spaceships from the earth were leaving, going to out space. As that sight, the colonel said with relieve, "Butcher, we human being, are having a war with you Swallowers. Our civilization can't be ruined by other species." Butcher's face turned red. He finally knew he had been tricked. Suddenly, he fell down because the ground of the moon started trembling. The colonel handed him a MacBook Air, on which the orbit of the moon was shown. The moon was heading straight to the Swallowers!

Butcher stood alone for a few minutes, murmuring, "You

cheated for years!" Suddenly, his eyes glared at the colonel monstrously and evilly. He swung his paw, and roared to the air, as if he was crazy. He roared, "Evil bugs, the swallowers never lie, even if sometimes we are cruel. However, you human beings, plan to kill us by lying." In great anger, he tried to use his giant paws to crash the colonel, but the colonel said calmly, "No time for fighting, Butcher. Let's leave the moon quickly as the nuclear is exploding."

Butcher left, and so did the colonel. The moon was in the orbit of reaching the tyre by the energy of nuclear. The swallowers fired lots of missiles attacking the moon, but soon, they gave up, since the missiles weren't powerful enough to destroy the moon.

On the earth, everybody was cheering, because they knew that the colonel's plan was working well, and the swallowers had to face their doom.

The colonel returned to his spaceship, and from there he saw the dazzling light of the moon. He laughed, and the sound of nuclear explosion was like music, the sweetest music he has even heard, or like water in the desert. The laughter contained all the joys from ancient to present, since he thought that earth would exist from the greatest invaders they knew in the universe.

The moon continued heading to the Swallowers. Suddenly something was very shocking happened. A part of the tyre separated willingly, heading to the moon. The colonel froze. The swallowers were planning to sacrifice that part in order to save the tyre!

The colonel opened the telescope on the spaceship. Through it, he saw that there were several swallowers on the part of the tyre. All of them were busy working. From their faces, the colonel saw sadness, but no fear. The colonel closed his eyes, until a small but vivid booming sound came into his ears. He knew that was the fate of the human being---The plan failed, and the earth would be destroyed.

Human failed, the colonel and his army knew it. However, during the fight against the Swallowers, they did everything they could do, even if they failed, that was still a glory. They accepted the invisible medal, they deserved it.

100 years later

The colonel landed on earth. Ruins everywhere, no sign of life, it was deadly silent. Surprisingly, he found out that there was still water. He tasted it, and it was not too salty. Suddenly, he heard a sound made by a spaceship, it was Butcher. "You are still alive! You have to be hundreds year old!" the colonel said. "No, I slept 10 years after the war, and I just woke up, only for meeting you again." Butcher answered.

"Where are you fellow swallowers? Are they leaving the

solar system?"

"Yes, they are reaching Uranus, and I'm going to chase them today." "There is still water and air left on the earth, is that a mercy of the Swallowers?"

Butcher shook his head, "There is nothing to do with mercy. The Swallowers were deeply damaged. We had to rebuild the lost part, and that took long, so we had little time to eat earth. Colonel, I know that in your heart, we Swallowers are devils, but you don't know when we made the decision of eating earth, we moaned and cried."

Butcher looked at the sun, he said, "Human beings, both you and we are the children of the sun, and earth is our home. The fathers of the Swallowers existed on earth 140 million years before your appearance. Furthermore, we created delightful civilizations."

The sea beside them reflected golden sunlight; the lava on the new-created hills flowed slowly. The two creatures who both has ruled earth, met each other.

Butcher continued, "Yes, we are dinosaurs. You human being think we died out because of meteorites, but the truth was we left the earth because we were overpopulated, and earth couldn't support us. You may ask why we destroy our home planet again, and the answer is: We have to survive. We have travelled in space for millions of years; home is nothing to us compare to our lives. Swallowers now are similar to a fish in a drying pond; we must leap forward before the pond dries. We also have to face the fate that we may die during the leap."

Butcher took out a bag, which was filled with mud. He said, "Colonel, you can go with us, since we respect you so much." He looked at the grass in the mud, and sighed, "After we left, the grasses will be the only life on earth."

The colonel hesitated. He looked at the mud under his feet. Suddenly, something caught his eyes, it was ants.

The colonel said, "Farewell, Butcher. I tried all my life to defend my home. We human being are not like you dinosaurs. We love our homeland and I will not abandon it. I'm old and my body is broken. Look at these ants; they will become rulers of this planet. I'll give my body to them."

Butcher left, but the colonel stayed. He laid on the ground, and breathed peacefully. The night fell, the sun drowned in the sea; stars blinked in the sky. This night was the most peaceful one ever.

In this night, earth was reborn.

"I'm the master of my fate" --- the story of Sam

A long time ago before the existence of human being, there were only two things in the universe, the good spirit and evil spirit. They swiveled round and round. Finally, they combined and became spirit balls. When God created human, he put a ball in each of them, which was the soul. God was too busy in working to notice that a spirit ball was still free. It sucked more and more energy into its own body and became very powerful. When God grasped this ball and out of curiosity he found it was different from others. In order to prevent it from becoming a threat, he separated it into two parts, a good half and an evil half. He put the evil half into his locker and used a spell promising to destroy it after ten years. God planned giving the good half to a child who had the most kind-hearted parents. Among the people he was creating, he picked a newly born boy whose name was Sam.

Suddenly God felt hungry, and he left. His elf assistant, Bob came with a bottle of wine. He was drunk. By mistake, he put the good half in the locker and set the evil half into Sam's soul.

Seven years passed. Sam was well known because he was so special. Everybody knew that he was a monster since he was controlled by evil, so they all avoided him. His family became poor since his parents had to compensate others again and again because Sam continued to destroy other's stuff. However, they never complained and their love for Sam never changed. Sam was sad and confused in the meantime since he couldn't control himself.

Bob saw what happened to Sam and felt very guilty. He decided to help.

Bob came to Sam's house and told Sam's father, "It's me who made your son an evil. I ask for forgiveness, and a chance to make amendment. Sam is doomed to die after three years. There is a slight chance to avoid the curse if the good half is found so that the good can mix with the evil." Sam's parents cried for their son's fate but agreed with no hesitation for letting Sam to travel with Bob for the good half. Before they left, Sam's father gave Sam a small necklace with a pendant. He told Sam, "Wherever you go, keep it on your neck, since it contains love from your parents."

After Bob and Sam began their journey, villagers spread the information out. Soon everybody knew "evil Sam" was coming. When Sam reached a village, everybody screamed and ran away. Sam was so upset. Bob didn't say anything but only patted him on the shoulder and took out the most delicious cake to Sam. Suddenly, Sam felt something warm in his heart. He has never got that feeling before. He tried to know what that was but he failed.

The next day, they entered the other village, and it was deadly silence. Suddenly, an old man appeared. Surprisingly, he asked Sam, "Are you the evil child?" He looked at Sam attentively, as if he was going to peek through Sam's body. He added, "You don't look evil. You can play with my grandsons." This attracted Sam a lot more than the delicious cake. When Sam played with the children and saw them laughing, the feeling of yesterday suddenly appeared, and it was clearer. Out of his habit, Sam wanted to hit the children, but a strange power stopped him. That was connected with the feeling just now. Later on Sam told Bob about what happened in his thought. Bob said nothing but the smile on his face showed the confidence on the finding the good half.

Three years went as fast as a blink in Sam's eyes. That strange feeling happened more and more often, which made Sam less violent and evil. One day, a cave appeared. They went in and saw the good half levitated there, still and peaceful. Wild with joy, Sam couldn't believe his eyes. The next day was the doomed day. They made it narrowly! Sam's eyes filled with tears and he looked at Bob questionably. Bob said gently, "Go and get it". Sam raced to the ball, and tried to grab it. However, the ball was like a phantom, and Sam's hand went right through it.

Sam tried and tried, but every time he failed. A voice echoed, "I will never be seized by anyone who has evil in his heart." Sam broke down with tears running. Bob patted him. Midnight came; Sam was exhausted and fell into sleep.

A picture appeared. Bob was talking to his father, "There is another way to save Sam, which is one of his beloved die by the curse in the doomed day." His father kneeled down before Bob immediately, he sobbed, "Let me replace him. Please save my kid." Afterwards, Sam saw

Bob gave his father a piece of paper, and his father put it in the pendent of the necklace.

Sam suddenly woke up. He slowly took off the necklace and opened the pendent. A piece of paper appeared and there was many spells on it. He read it slowing. He murmured," Thank you, Dad, for your love. A man should never surrender to his fate, no matter good or bad. I'll face the destruction myself." When the first shot of sunlight peered through the forest, Sam tore the spell gravely and waited calmly for his doom to come.

Suddenly, he felt something moving behind him. He turned around and found the good half was moving slowly towards him. When the ball collided with his body, red lights burst out. The curse came! With a lightning, the evil half was destroyed. Sam fainted. A few minute later on, he woke up and found the good half was already in his body.

Sam was reborn and became a hero later on.

The age of angels

On the international science conference:

"Let's welcome Dr. T to give a speech. As everyone knows, he was awarded Nobel Prize 11 years ago because of his outstanding contribution on genetic engineering. Today, he comes here to show his new achievement. Welcome." The president of the association said.

Dr. T is a Tanzanian. He is short and pale since in his childhood; no nutritional food was produced for him and all the other children. His eyes sink deeply into the eye pits; his body is always hunched, and he is very sensitive, even the sound made by a pin dropped on the ground can make him nervous. He walks slowly onto the stage, and with his special, slow voice, he speaks.

"Ladies and gentlemen, to tell everyone the truth, in the first several years after I got the Nobel Prize, I was working on the genetic engineering of plants. My goal, at first, was to rebuild the gene of some edible plants, such as crops and beans, in order to solve the food shortage in Tanzania. In my childhood, the food was not enough for every child. Being a Tanzanian, I think I have the ability to help every one of the kids in Tanzania, even the kids from all the poor places in the world."

Thundering applauses lingered around everyone's ears. "Did you succeed?" one of the scientists asks.

"No, I didn't." Dr. T says in a deep and sad voice. "I tried for a long time, working every day and night, but nothing was achieved. Tanzania is so infertile that the plants are still not able to be planted even if I have already changed their genes.

"So, what do you really discover, or have done, and want to share with us today, Dr?" The same scientist asks.

"In the sixth year, I was actually puzzled. What is the way

to solve this problem? At that time, this problem is unsolvable. I did my best to change the gene of plants, but it still didn't work. I was thinking about it no matter day or night. However, suddenly, I discovered that I was working on the wrong way. I think if we can't defeat the nature, let's join it. If rebuilding plants' gene cannot succeed, then I can rebuild humans' gene. In this case, the hell for regular people may be the heaven for changed ones."

Dr. T turns to the right side, and a black boy comes on the stage. This boy is strong and tall. When he stands beside Dr. T, the huge difference is shocking. Dr. T's voice begins, "This is Kardo, a Tanzanian boy. Now, I will show you his life." He snaps his fingers, and a bunch of leaves are sent to the stage. Kardo grabs these leaves and sends them into his mouth and smiles happily. Dr. T says, "That is what I mean by 'joining' the nature. Change the gene of men to make them easy to survive. By re-building human's gene, every child in the poor families can get enough food and can stay away from hunger."

Dr. T walks down the stage slowly and sits down. The whole room is deadly silent, and everybody seems to be frozen. A soft and calm voice appears, that is from the president of the association.

"Arrest them, both Dr. T and Kardo." He says, but when he realizes the guards are not moving, he suddenly cries out crazily, "Arrest them! Don't care about the foreign immunity! It is for human, not devil. They are devils, the devils from the hell! Arrest them, be quick, do I have to say the third time?"

The American president speaks, "Dr. T, you may get Nobel Prize for the second time, but you have made yourself the enemy of all the civilized countries. Well, since you are the initiator, I think we should send you back to Tanzania to warn the local government that if Tanzania doesn't expel all of the creatures like Kardo, Tanzania will be under the attack of all the civilized countries."

Dr. T is calm. "Don't be nervous." He says. "I will send the message. Now, I have to go back to Tanzania to do the things that you guys told me to do."

A few days later, the civilized world is crazy. Everyone, everywhere is criticizing Tanzania, describing them as Satan from the lowest level of the hell. Everyone is calling for destroying Tanzania and capture Dr. T to stop this crazy movement. In their eyes, rebuilding human's gene is against humanity.

The day for the Tanzanians to bring out the changed comes. All the high officers in the civilized world are gathering at the harbor, looking for a boat carrying Dr. T and the changed.

A boat slowly comes. Dr. T is standing on the deck. He

seems to be young. His back is not bended and body is not hunched. In his face appears confidence. When the boat is boarded, Dr. T walks to the high officers with a crowd of Tanzanians with black robes in the back.

"The officers of the civilized countries, I take the changed here, but before I hand them to you, I want to say something."

"No matter in which period of time or which place in the history, stay away from hunger and be alive is the most essential need. Other things do not appear to be so important. Tanzania is facing the problem of hunger. We have to do something to change this situation since we cannot let hunger destroy Tanzania."

He continues, smiling at the officers, "I, not only solve the problem of hunger, but also achieve everyone's dream, which is flying. Although the civilized countries don't have the problem of hunger, no one can resist the temptation of flying, which has been the dream from the existence of human. "

Ignoring the astonishing eyes looking at him, he says, "The age of human has passed, and the age of angels has come!"

In the back of Dr. T, the robed men take off their robe, and wings appear on the back. When they fly, the sky is covered by the wings absolute white…

The age of angels has begun!

The Learning Machine

It was over midnight. Tom was still studying hard. He was the best student of the whole grade. To keep this, he must spend more time on learning, which meant the sacrifice of his sleeping. Watching the exercise books and papers, he felt anxiety and lonely, "What if I become the second best? I can't bear it. I have to do something." Tom stared at the moon outside the house. He thought for the way to solve this problem the whole night. When the sun rose, he figured something out. A secret and mysterious smile appeared on his face.

Everything was usual these days, except one thing, which is Tom often locked himself in his room, without eating or drinking, and some strange noise often came outside from his room. His parents were curious but since Tom was a good boy, so they chose not to bother him.

One day, a scream came from Tom's room. "I finally make it, the potion of knowledge." His parents came to his room and asked, "What is it?" Tom said, "Nothing at all, but just something useful for me. Don't worry."

When the night came, Tom secretly got up. Knowing the potion could make him get high scores at any time, his eyes were shinning, lips moving, and several words came out of his mouth, "High scores and champions of any competition." With trembling hands, he slowly put the potion beneath his lips, and then, drank it.

Days flew peacefully till the math competition started. Once Tom grasped his pencil, answers poured out in his mind. He never stopped, and he finished doing this paper in ten minutes. When the teacher was checking Tom's paper, his mouth opened in a big O! What is this??!!

After drinking the potion, Tom was the best in any test every time, and he could answer all of the questions, fast and without any mistake. However, when time went by, everybody noticed Tom's change.

One day, one of his classmates poured water on Tom's book accidentally. "I'm really sorry, Tom. I can help you to dry your book," he said. Tom had no expression, but only looked at him coldly. When that boy tried to dry Tom's book, Tom suddenly pushed him on the ground and hit him hard. After that, he just walked away and left the boy stunned and surprise. "Why is Tom so cruel now?"

The other day, his mom was sick after eating some oysters and shrimps. Mom said, "Tom, can you bring me a cup of hot water with medicine, I feel dizzy now." However, Tom just sat in his room without moving and pretending not hearing it. "Tom, Tom…." She called, but still no response. Mom felt very sad and she thought, "Tom is a sweet boy and always cares me a lot. Why is he doing such thing today, which is breaking my heart?"

Similar things happened again and again. His Mom felt painful about his changing. "What makes such a good boy change to be so cold-blooded?" One night, his Mom slowly walked out of her room, with the moonlight, she tiptoed into Tom's room without been noticed. Tom was lying peacefully in the bed like a baby. This reminded his mom of the cute boy in the old time. But suddenly, something attracted her. It was a sound coming out of Tom's mouth, saying some mathematic equations and English words. Mom leaned forward to clarify, but suddenly, she screamed and step backwards, because she found out Tom's belly shining red. Tom was already awake. He smiled automatically and said, "You finally found out, mom. Actually, that potion had side-effect, which is making people expressionless, in other word, acting as a robot." He pointed at his stomach. "But it can get my record better. I care nothing else except my studies…"

Dear readers, when you walk on the streets, can you tell who Tom is? Actually, there are many Toms around us. Do you think it is worthy giving up everything for scores?

THE FINALE

A Lesson

The Tortoise and the Hare

Everyone knows the story "The tortoise and the hare" in Aesop's fable. It is mainly about a running race between a tortoise and a hare. The hare is fast, and the tortoise is slow; however, the hare becomes proud and sleeps in the race while the tortoise continues running. Finally, the tortoise surpasses the hare and wins the race. What can we learn from this story? In my opinion, we can learn that don't be proud when you are in prosperity and don't give up in adversity.

The first thing we can learn is never be too proud. You may be good, but you cannot be too proud in any moment. In this story, the hare is over confident since the tortoise runs slowly; however, it is the proud that makes the hare lose the game. Therefore, no matter what situation you are in, what distance is between you and your opponent, stay foolish and remain humble. Always remember that your opponent has a possibility of surpassing you. In my school, I am that hare, for my score is often the highest in the class, or even in the grade. In the final test of grade five, I got the highest score in the grade. I became very proud and did not learn hard in the summer vacation because of the high score. When the school started again, one of my schoolmates, who I beat in the final test of grade five, surpassed me in the first test of grade six. From this example, we can see being too proud will make you be surpassed.

We all know that the hare runs fast and the tortoise runs slowly, but the tortoise doesn't give up. It keeps on running and finally catches up with the hare. However, if the tortoise abandons when he sees the hare running fast, no matter the hare is running or sleeping, the tortoise can never catch up with the hare. Therefore, the second point I want to say is never give up. Life is a long race, and you will face many opponents. Some run faster than you; some run slower than you. However, always remember that the ones who are fast may not be able to keep that speed; the ones who are slow may be fast later. There is English saying that he who laughs last, laughs best. The ones who succeed are always the ones who keep on trying and never give up. I was in a group that gathers the best 100 students in math in the whole city. There, I was the tortoise in the beginning since I ranked 98 in the test. However, I kept on trying and didn't give up. Finally,

I surpassed most of the students and ranked 9.

As I've said, life is a long journey. You may be a hare, but you can also be a tortoise. When you are a hare, don't be proud; when you are a tortoise, don't give up. Keep on trying, and you will be the best version of yourself.